TEN POEMS AND LYRICS BY MAO TSE-TUNG

毛主席詩詞

手稿十首

Ten Poems and Lyrics
by Mao Tse-tung

Translation and woodcuts
by Wang Hui-Ming

University of Massachusetts Press   Amherst 1975

English text and woodcut copyright (c) 1975 by Wang Hui-Ming

Library of Congress Catalog Card Number 74-21248

ISBN 0-87023-178-2 (cloth); 0-87023-182-0 (paper)

Designed by Richard Hendel

Set in IBM Pyramid by Cecelia May

Printed in the United States of America

Versions of "Changsha," "Loushan Pass," and "Inscription on a Photograph" first appeared in *American Poetry Review*, 3, no. 3, 1974.

Publisher's note: The Chinese text of this volume, including reproductions of the calligraphy of Mao Tse-tung, was originally published in the People's Republic of China. Reproduction herein is not by arrangement with the original publisher and author, since no formal arrangements have been effected between their government and that of the United States of America, as of the date of publication of this edition.

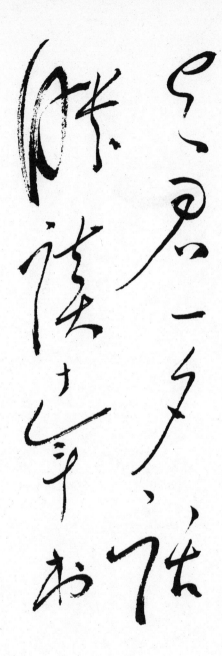

For Robert Francis

whose life and poetry
would win the admiration
of Chairman Mao and to
whom I say, "Chatting
with you for one evening
is better than reading for
ten years."

Contents

Chairman Mao as a young poet.

Introduction

This book is based on *Ten Poems and Lyrics* by *Chairman Mao*, published by Tung Fang Hung Press, Shanghai, in 1969. The character text is the same as in *Chairman Mao's Poems and Lyrics,* published by the People's Literature Press in September 1966. The word "lyric" is used here as a translation of the Chinese character *t'zu,* a collective term for a particular style of poetry expressly written to fit a melody. These ten poems cover a time span of almost half a century starting in 1922. Each poem is a narrative of a historic incident in the Chinese Revolution. No effort was made to ascertain the exact date of each poem except to translate the date in the colophon whenever it appears in Mao's original calligraphy, which is also included in this book.

Chinese characters were in ancient times picture-ideas, and some characters still are. A Chinese poem has always been a word-painting, be this painting visual or mental. Unlike any other written language, the Chinese character is more than just an action word; its structural elements sometimes relate to each other to form a picture of ideas. By the same token, characters in a poem act graphically to weave an imagined tapestry of poetic situations without relying heavily on grammatical conventions or syntax as long as the visual structure of the poem is in focus. Sound makes the poem a word-picture-time-music. Unfortuantely, there is no way to reproduce this music in translation, other than the inadequate method of romanization.

When I make this general observation, I am fully aware of the controversial issues involved in translating Chinese poetry into English, with Fenollosa and Pound on the one side and George Kennedy and other linguists on the other. I respect and understand their views, but I cannot wholly subscribe to all their learned opinions. In art, the whole is greater than the sum of its parts. Dissecting a character into separate parts to search for the total meaning of a poem in translation is in most cases just as farfetched as a total denial that the basic principle of picture-ideas underlying the structure of Chinese characters has any bearing whatsoever on the selection of characters by the poet. Should I be suspected of borrowing ideas from Fenollosa, this suspicion is skin deep, for our similarity is only in terminology. Art comes from convention and not invention. My sympathy lies with the Chinese convention that there must be painting in poetry and poetry in painting. In other words, I would like to see a poem written with a painter's eyes and a painting painted with a poet's mind.

With these points in mind, I shall do the following in the book: (1) romanize the characters in the Wade-Giles system, (2) render the text word by word into an appropriate English equivalent, (3) literally translate the line, and (4) translate the poem as a whole. Hopefully, this will reveal the thinking process of a translator whose native language is Chinese. As for points 2 and 3, some readers may feel that there could be better choices of words for the rendition and literal translation. But I have reasons for doing what I did: to use the most common English words in the rendition to retain the accuracy and simplicity of characters in the original poem; and to translate literally, as close as possible to the Chinese word order, thus revealing the changes from literal to free translation. I do not want to rely on English grammar and syntax to dilute the impact of the original Chinese line. The best way to read Chinese poetry is to try to think Chinese. Translation based on this principle sometimes reads awkwardly, but there is no way to avoid it. For instance, in the poem "Changsha," Mao used *wan shan* ("ten thousand mountains" or "hills") and *ch'ang-k'ung* ("long void" or "endless empty" for the air or the sky). We know the usages here of *wan* and *ch'ang* mean more than just "ten thousand" and "long"; the Chinese have their own way of using numerical characters, and I would like to see the readers have a chance to find out for themselves. In the same poem, Mao used two characters together, *wan* ("ten thousand") and *lei* ("kind" or "sort"); these could be translated as "myriad species," but I prefer to stick to "ten thousand kind," because "kind" is more inclusive, applicable to both animate and inanimate objects in the context of the poem. It is better to translate *wan lei* as "everything," which is accurately vague, as it is in the original.

When a Western student learns Chinese, he learns to read from a book and seldom learns to write with a brush at the same time, as a Chinese pupil does in his early childhood. As a result, while he may be able to read Chinese in printed books, he may not be able to read a handwritten personal letter from his Chinese friend. Since he cannot write with a brush, the full beauty of calligraphy forever eludes him. He knows that he should like calligraphy as a form of art, but he will never be able to feel an emotional affinity with what he calls "the brush work." Mao's calligraphy was evolved from *k'aishu* (regular script), which was in use before the 1949 revolution, and not from the simplified characters as shown in this text, which are currently used throughout China. But a student who has learned to write with a brush and is familiar with the stroke order of any style of *k'aishu* will find no difficulty in tracing the kinship of Mao's calligraphy to either regular style or simplified *k'aishu*. Technically speaking, Mao's calligraphy is a combination of *ts'aoshu* (grass writing or cursive script) and *hsingshu* (running writing or script), a beautiful combination in expression of individuality. We shall not go into details about the evolution of Chinese calligraphic styles except to say that both the grass and the running styles are a carefree handwritten style for daily use, and sometimes, at a higher level, they are used for artistic expression. Reference to *ts'aoshu* as grass writing or script is actually an error in translation. *Ts'ao* by itself means "grass," but in the compound, *ts'aoshu*, it means "rough," "hurried," or "carefree"; *shu* by itself means "book" or "writing," but here it means "the way of writing" or "draft." Thus, *ts'aoshu* really means a "rough draft," which is exactly what Mao's calligraphy is. To wit: in line six of the poem "The Long March," Mao squeezed the character for "chain," *so*, by the side of the word *t'ieh* ("iron") instead of placing it between the words *t'ieh* and *han* as it should be. This indicates that he missed the word *so* when he first wrote it and subsequently corrected his mistake. But in art, neatness bows to expressiveness; it is not important to squeeze the missing word in proper order. Furthermore, if one looks carefully at the two dots at the bottom of the character *han*, one can see that he wrote the scroll casually with a worn-out brush and with the speed and zest of an action painter but that his expressiveness came from long and arduous practice. The writing bears a studied ease like that of a prima donna in action It is accurate, free, and spirited and has what master calligraphers call "muscle, bone, blood, and flesh." By "muscle," they mean the correct use of the wrist, which gives posture and poise to the character; "bone" furnishes the structural strength to the writing; "blood" comes from the choice of water; and "flesh" from the correct density of the ink. The movement of the stroke and the vitality of the execution breathe life into the beauty of Mao's calligraphy. Calligraphy stands high among all arts in China. It is direct in action and pure in conception. It is nondescriptive and nonspecific. It cannot be associated with any recognizable object, and it stands by itself. One stroke begins the origin of all existence, and one root forms the roots of all forms.

In Mao's calligraphy, we can see that he is a man of firm determination, unpredictable mood, quick in decision and fast in action—soft yet strong, pliable yet penetrating, sophisticated yet earthy, and delicate yet robust. In short, he is indeed a "simplicated" and "complified" man. The upward tilt of the right corner of his characters suggests a contempt of conventions. It is reminiscent of the calligraphy by the eccentric poet, essayist, painter, and seal artist Cheng Hsien (1683-1765), who called himself *feng tzu* ("the mad man").

Both men show an unyielding independence in their work, a quality treasured by all and achieved by few in the history of art.

When I read English translations of Chinese poetry, I often wonder how the translator's mind works. Sometimes I feel like a man scratching his back with a shirt on: the itch is not really quenched. My poetic itch is covered by the shirt of translation. Then I realize that what the translator did was to translate what he thought the poet meant rather than what the poet said. For instance, in the last line of the first stanza in the poem "Changsha," the words *ch'en* ("to sink") and *fu* ("to float") have been translated as "fate," "destiny," or even "nature." Any of these may be what Mao meant, but they are not what he said. He actually said, "I ask the awesome great earth who masters [or determines] the sinking and floating." Now, suppose we know a young poet standing by a riverside, near a lake, looking at a magnificent landscape with hundreds of boats racing on the water, with a burning desire for revolution running high in his blood, asking, "Who is to determine the sinking and floating?" How could he mean anything but the "fate" of man or the "destiny" of a nation? But why should the translator interpret what he said into abstract words such as "fate" and "destiny," rather than faithfully translate his action words, *ch'en* and *fu*, into "sinking" and "floating?" This would not only be unfaithful to the poet but would also insult the intelligence of the reader. At the other extreme, we have translators who forget that poetic translation is for poetry and not for dictionary definition. When I translated *wan hu hou* into "the lords of the land," I was accused of inaccuracy, and one of the mushrooming scholars in "Chinese Studies" suggested that I should have stuck to the Han dynasty (206 B.C.-A.D. 220) term, "the marquis of ten thousand families." In the first place, the title "marquis," the man in charge of the marches on border regions, which was first bestowed in England in 1386, is at best a very rough equivalent of the ancient Han term *hou*, a feudal prince, "the man who was first in rank." A Chinese man who was first in rank (*hou*) preceded an English man who controlled the border patrol (marquis) by approximately one thousand years in time and heaven knows how many steps in rank. Secondly, when Mao wrote the poem in 1926, China had been a republic for more than a decade and those glorious "marquises" had been dead more than two thousand years. "Lords of the land" was quite fitting to the situation in China, which at that time was infested with villainous warlords and big land owners with private armies who lorded over the people. I tried to avoid using the clumsy mouthful, "marquises of ten thousand families." Some sinologists tend to forget that what is good for the dictionary is not necessarily good for poetry. In other cases, when Mao used a simple and accurate word, some translators would substitute a fancier word with connotations they thought would fit their concept of Oriental art. For instance, the Chinese word *ou* means "bowl," and when Mao used a broken "golden bowl" to symbolize war-torn China, it became a "golden vase" in the hands of certain translators. The word "bowl" carries an unwritten allusion to rice and by extension to land, whereas the word "vase" suggests the lustrous decorative Ming porcelain which was enjoyed only by rich landlords and decadent mandarins. Would the great revolutionary poet Mao use an art object from the controlling class to symbolize the war-torn and starving country? When the history-conscious Mao wrote his own lines, he must have remembered the statement made by Emperor Wu (A.D.420-23 of the Sung dynasty House of Liu) in *The History of South*, "My country is strong and solid like a golden bowl, there is not a single crack or flaw in it," and the line, "my country is fully plenteous like a golden bowl" in a poem by Sung Chiung. In the same poem, Mao wrote, *fen t'ien fen ti* (to "share field and land"); in translation the phrase became "redistribution of land." "Redistribution" does not cover the whole gamut of connotations in the history of Chinese peasant rebellions and attempted land reforms, such as the ancient "well field system," the Taiping Rebellion in the nineteenth century, and the 1906 insurrection in Mao's native province Hunan led by his fellow Hunanese, Huang Hsing, whom he had greatly admired when he arrived at Changsha in September, a month before the 1911 revolution, the revolution that changed China from an empire into a republic. On the banners of these uprisings were the words, *fen t'ien* or *fen ti*. Here the word *fen* not only means "division" and "redistribution" of the land but also means "sharing" the labor, the harvest, the hopes and despairs, and all the other ups and downs that go with collective farming. The ownership of the land in this context does not even seem to be important. To redistribute may be more "scientific," current, and legalistic, but to "share" is more moral and human. This is what the Chinese Revolution is about.

Most Chinese poetry is written in simple characters, and one does not need a large vocabulary to appreciate it. After all, there are only somewhat more than a thousand characters in the great *Tao Te Ching*, and most of them are common characters. A student in elementary Chinese can read Chinese poetry without difficulty if the poetry is presented to him as a word-picture. In fact, he will enjoy it more and learn faster if he begins his reading in poetry and writing with a brush instead of learning Chinese as a tool to learn other things Chinese later, as commonly practiced today in universities. The very attitude of learning a language as a tool dulls the sense of wonder and diminishes the pleasure of learning. The following is an example of the way I would like to see Chinese poetry presented to the students:

Ch'ü nien chin jih tz'u men chung

去年今日此门中

Gone/year/to-/day/this/door/in

Last year today in this door

Jen mien t'ao hua hsiang ying hung

人面桃花相映紅

Human/face/peach/flower/mutual, reciprocal/shine, reflect/red

Human face peach flower mutual shine red

Jen mien pu chih ho ch'u ch'ü

人面不知何处去

Human/face/not/know/what/place/go

Human face not know where go

T'ao hua i,yi chiu hsiao ch'un feng

桃花依归笑春風

Peach/flower/as/old/smile/spring/wind

Peach flower as before smile spring wind

A year ago today in this gate,
Her face, like the peach blossom, ruddied radiance
I know not where she has gone, but
Peach flowers as always smile in the spring breeze.

If I recall correctly, this is probably one of Yuan Mei's (1716-79) early poems. Yuan Mei was a romantic, hot-tempered, witty, and generous poet who could express the deepest feeling with simplest words. And he formed, in his precocious adolescence, a lifelong habit of "asking for flowers and seeking for willows" (chasing beautiful women). This poem was about his annual trip to the countryside on Ching Ming Day (a spring festival, celebrated by flying kites, strolling in the countryside, and sniffing wild flowers). That was the reason he used exact time words in the first line. Why did I choose the word "gate" rather than "door" for the Chinese character *men*, which in most cases is translated as "door"? Because the Chinese village is usually surrounded by a mud wall with a thatched-roof-covered gate facing the road, and the poet wanted readers to know that the girl was out of her house, about to come out of the gate, and unexpectedly met the glance of a handsome stranger who "flirted with her with his eyes." Do I stretch my imagination too far? Not if we know the colloquial expression, *t'iao pang tzu*, in Yuan Mei's native place. *T'iao pang tzu* (flirtation with eyes) is slang, a little obscure in origin but poetic in meaning, used to describe the expressions in the eyes of young lovers at their first meeting, before they speak to each other. All this unsaid poetry is implied in the word *men*, which in this case could be translated only as "gate," not "door." If she were inside a door, he could not have seen her through the mud wall. For Chinese readers, *men* would be good enough to convey the thought-picture; we do not have to make a distinction between a door and a gate. The key characters in this poem are *hsiang* ("mutual, reciprocal"), *ying* ("shine, reflect"), and *hung* ("red"); the action word is *ying*. Together they form a thought of "shining red mutually with the peach blossom." Would an English line, "Her face ruddied radiance like the peach blossom," be adequate to express this complicated thought? I leave the reader to judge. How exciting it would be if a student could have a chance to better this translation with his own English by following the same thinking process. He learns poetry and Chinese at the same time.

Being neither a student of language nor a poet, I claim no erudition in linguistic niceties or poetic preciosities. I say what I have to say as a painter and calligrapher who loves Chinese poetry and sees it as a graphic presentation of a poetic situation. The presence of this poetic-graphic situation (word-painting) is a necessary ingredient in translation. When Robert Frost quipped that poetry is what disappears in translation, could he have meant the absence of this poetic-graphic situation?

I realize that it is less sinful to write bad poems than to translate good ones badly. If Mao's poetry comes through my translation, credit must go to him as a good poet. If readers find flaws, no one but I am to blame. Finally, I must thank Mrs. Franklin W. Houn for her bravery in checking my romanization.

Wang Hui-Ming

Ch'ang-sha

长沙

Long-sand
Changsha

Tu　li　han　ch'iu

独 立 寒 秋 ，

Alone/stand/cold/autumn
Stand alone in autumn cold

Hsiang　chiang　pei　ch'ü

湘 江 北 去 ，

Hsiang/river/north/go
The Hsiang River flows northward

Chü-tzu　chou　t'ou

橘 子 洲 头 。

Orange/islet/head
On the tip of Islet Orange

K'an　wan　shan　hung　pien

看 万 山 红 遍 ，

Look/ten thousand/mountain/red/everywhere
Look at ten thousand mountains, red everywhere

Ts'eng lin chin jan

层 林 尽 染；

Layer/forest/all/stain
The layers of forest all stained

Man chiang pi t'ou

漫 江 碧 透，

Overflow/river/green/transparent
The overflowing river transparent green

Pai ko cheng liu

百 舸 争 流。

Hundred/giant boats/compete/current
Hundreds of giant boats sail against the current

Ying chi ch'ang-k'ung

鹰 击 长 空，

Eagles/strike/long-void, sky
Eagles soar in the air

Yü hsiang ch'ien ti

鱼 翔 浅 底，

Fish/soar, glide/shallow/bottom
Fish swim in the shallow bottom

10

Wan lei shuang t'ien ching tzu-yu

万类霜天竞自由。

Ten thousand/kind/frost/sky/pursue/freedom
Everything under the frosty sky pursues freedom

Ch'ang liao-k'uo

怅寥廓，

Disappoint/dome of heaven
Bewildered by vast space

Wen ts'ang-mang ta ti

问苍茫大地，

Ask/vast, awesome/big/earth
Ask the awesome great earth

Shei chu ch'en fu

谁主沉浮？

Who/master/sink/float
Who is master of the sinking and floating

Hsieh lai pai lü ts'eng yu

携来百侣曾游。

Bring/come/hundred/companion/past/visit
I brought hundreds of companions to visit

Yi wang-hsi cheng-yung sui-yüeh ch'ou

忆 往 昔 峥 嵘 岁 月 稠。

Remember/past/lofty/times/crowded
Remember the past lofty, fast-growing days

Ch'ia t'ung-hsüeh shao-nien

恰 同 学 少 年，

Just then/schoolmate/youth
Just young schoolmates

Feng hua cheng mao

风 华 正 茂；

Wind/flower/just then/flourish
Flowery bud just flourishing

Shu-sheng yi-ch'i

书 生 意 气，

Scholar/rightness
Righteous scholars

Hui ch'ih fang ch'iu

挥 斥 方 遒。

Shake/scold/square/strong, unyielding
Shake and scold squarely and vigorously

Chih tien chiang-shan

指 点 江 山，

Finger/point/landscape
Point finger at landscape

Chi yang wen tzu

激 扬 文 字，

Stir/rise/writing/word
Stir and excite writing and speech

Fen t'u tang-nien wan-hu-hou

粪 土 当 年 万 户 侯。

Dung/dirt/in the past/duke of 10,000 households
Dung and dirt in the past, landlord of 10,000 farmer households

Ts'eng chi fou

曾 记 否，

[Indicates past action]/remember/not
Do you not remember

Tao chung liu chi shui

到 中 流 击 水，

Reach/mid/current/strike/water
We reached the midstream and struck the water

Lang   o   fei   chou

浪 遏 飞 舟？

Wave/impede/fly/boat

Waves crashed against the flying boat

Changsha

Alone, standing in autumn cold
As the Hsiang River flows north
Past the tip of Island Orange,
I see red hills everywhere and
Forest after forest stained crimson.
The overflowing river is limpid green.
A hundred giant boats race against the current.
Eagles soar in the sky and
Fish glide in the shallows.
Everything under the frosty sky strives for freedom.
Bewildered by this vast space,
I ask the awesome great earth,
Who is to determine the sinking and floating?

I brought hundreds of companions to visit here
In those lusty, fast-growing days.
We were young schoolmates,
Flowering at the peak of splendor,
Fair-minded scholars,
Forthright and fearless.
Pointing at these hills and rivers,
Impetuous in words and writings,
We accused Lords of the Land as dung and dirt
For enslaving millions of farmers.

Do you remember?
When reaching midstream, we struck the water,
How the raging waves crashed against our flying boat.

Changsha is the capital city of Hunan Province, near where Mao was born. It is situated on the Hsiang River, which flows northward to Tungting Lake. In and around this city Mao spent his student days and developed a deep understanding of the land and people of China.

嵘岁月稠恰同学少年风华正茂书生意气挥斥方遒指点江山激扬文字粪土当年万户侯曾记否到中流击水浪遏飞舟

独立寒秋，湘江北去，橘子洲头。看万山红遍，层林尽染；漫江碧透，百舸争流。鹰击长空，鱼翔浅底，万类霜天竞自由。怅寥廓，问苍茫大地，谁主沉浮？

Throughout the translation, place names are spelled as on Chinese maps and by the Chinese postal service, e.g., Changsha, rather than Ch'angsha.

Many Chinese words are compounds of two or three characters, which are bound forms of expression. For the sake of simplicity, we do not analyze all of the characters etymologically. Thus, in the tenth line, *tzu* ("self")-*yu* ("will") is simply translated as "freedom," and *shao* ("less")-*nien* ("year"), as "youth." Sometimes the compounds are duplications of the same character, for emphasis or to fill the requirements of a certain poetic form. In such cases, we translate them as a single term. The character *tzu*, in the third line, by itself means "son," but usually it is attached to a noun as an anclitic, as in *chü-tzu*, "orange-son," which is translated as "Orange."

In line 7 *ko* means big boat. "Down South, in Hunan River Region, all big boats are called ko"—*On Dialect: The New Supplement to Shuo Wen*, a famous dictionary compiled about 80 B.C..

Huang   Ho   Lou

黄鹤楼

Yellow Crane Tower

Mang mang   Chiu   p'ai   liu   chung   kuo

茫茫 九 派 流 中 国 ，

Vast/nine/branch off/flow/middle/country
Nine immense tributaries flow in the center of the country

Ch'en ch'en   yi   hsien   ch'uan   nan   pei

沉 沉 一 线 穿 南 北 。

heavy/one/line/thread/south/north
One heavy line threads from south to north

Yen   yü   mang   ts'ang ts'ang

烟 雨 莽 苍 苍 ，

Smoke/rain/blue wide space/blue-grey infinite atmosphere
In the blue grey air of smoke and rain

Kuei   she   so   ta   chiang

龟 蛇 锁 大 江 。

Tortoise/snake/lock/big/river
Tortoise and Snake Hills guard the big river

Huang ho chih ho ch'ü

黄 鹤 知 何 去 ？

Yellow/crane/know/where/go
Who knows where the yellow crane goes

Sheng yu yu jen ch'u

剩 有 游 人 处 。

Remain/have/traveler/place
This traveler's place remains

Pa chiu lo t'ao t'ao

把 酒 酹 滔 滔 ，

Hold/wine/pour down/overflow, torrent
Pour down wine torrentially

Hsin ch'ao chu lang kao

心 潮 逐 浪 高 ！

Heart/tide/pursuit/wave/high
The tide in the heart matches the height of the wave

茫茫九派流中国，沉沉一线穿南北。烟雨莽苍苍，龟蛇锁大江。

黄鹤知何去？剩有游人处。把酒酹滔滔，心潮逐浪高。

调寄菩萨蛮

一九二七

The Yellow Crane Tower

Nine gigantic tributaries flow in the heartland of the country,
One heavy line threads from north to south.
Veiled in the blue haze of misty rain,
Tortoise Mountain and Snake Hill guard the mighty river.

Who knows where the yellow cranes have gone?
Only this wayfarer's place remains.
I pour down a torrent of wine for
The tide in my heart surges as high as the waves.   *1927*

The Yellow Crane Tower is a historic site on the bank of the Yangtze River
at Wuchang, which together with Hankow and Hanyang forms a tri-city center
of communication and industry in the center of China. This is also the place
where nine tributaries from Hunan and Hupeh provinces meet the Yangtze.
According to *The Romances of Three Kingdoms*, a novel about the period
A.D. 220-65, the leaders of the three warring states held a conference here to
reconcile their differences but failed to do so. The incident is celebrated in a
popular Peking opera with the same title as the poem.

"One heavy line" in the second line refers to the Peking-Kwangchow
(Canton) Railroad, which crosses over the Yangtze River through Wuchang
and Hankow. Snake Hill, on top of which the Yellow Crane Tower is situated,
is on the riverbank at Wuchang. Tortoise Hill stands on the opposite side, at
Hanyang.

The "yellow cranes," fifth line, may be the poet's allusion to the ancient
heroes who held a conference there.

Chung ("middle")-*kuo* ("country"), as a compound, is usually translated
as "China," but here, for the purpose of parallel construction and in contrast
to the second line, it seems more accurate to translate it as a geographic term,
the "center" or "heartland" of the country.

Mang-ts'ang ("blue infinite air," "open space") is a two-character compound,
but here again the poetic form demands three characters to complete a five-
beat line. Mao makes this possible by duplicating the second character of the
compound, *ts'ang.*

Chiang Kuei Chan Cheng

蒋桂战争

Chiang/Kwangsi/fight/contend
Chiang battles in Kwangsi

Feng yün t'u pien

风云突变，

Wind/cloud/sudden/change
Wind and cloud suddenly change

Chün-fa ch'ung k'ai-chan

军阀重开战。

Warlord/again/begin/fight
Warlords fight again

Sa hsiang jen-chien tu shih yüan

洒向人间都是怨，

Spread/toward/people's world/all/is/complain
Spreading suffering among the people

Yi chen huang liang tsai hsien

一枕黄粱再现。

One/pillow/yellow/grain/again/appear
One pillow of yellow grain reappears

Hung ch'i yüeh kuo Ting Chiang

红 旗 跃 过 汀 江 ,

Red/banner/leap/over/Ting/River
The red banners leap over the Ting River

Chih hsia Lung-yen Shang-hang

直 下 龙 岩 上 杭 。

Straight/down/Lungyen/Shanghang
Straight down toward Lungyen and Shanghang

Shou-shih chin ou yi p'ien

收 拾 金 瓯 一 片 ,

Pick up, repair/gold/bowl/one/piece
Pick up and repair a piece of gold bowl

Fen t'ien fen ti chen mang

分 田 分 地 真 忙 。

Divide/field/divide/land/real/busy
Divide the land and field really busy

Chiang Battles in Kwangsi

Suddenly the wind and clouds burst into storm,
The warlords are fighting again,
Spreading misery among the people.
A pillow of yellow grain emerges once more.

The red banners leap over the Ting River,
Straight down toward Lungyen and Shanghang.
Let's pick up and mend a piece of the golden bowl,
We will be busy sharing the land and the field.

While Chiang Kai-shek was fighting the warlords in Kwangsi, the Red Army advanced from Kiangsi toward Fukien and established a base in Fukien. Lungyen ("Dragon Rock") and Shanghang are two border towns in Fukien Province.

"A pillow of yellow grain," or as it is more commonly known, "a dream of yellow grain," is an allusion to a T'ang dynasty story of a poor scholar named Lu. Traveling in the western part of China, Lu met a Taoist monk who provided him with shelter. The monk took a pillow from his bag and said, "Sleep on this pillow, and your wish will come true." While the Taoist was cooking "yellow grain" (millet, a poor man's staple diet in northwest China) for supper, the scholar took a nap on the pillow. He dreamed that he married a beautiful woman who was a faithful wife and dutiful mother, and after passing the imperial examination, he was appointed the commander of garrison troops in the border region of western China, where he rose quickly to the lofty position of prime minister in the T'ang court. When he woke up, the millet wasn't even cooked. Surprised, he said, "Was I dreaming?" The monk smiled and said, "Isn't life a dream?" Mao uses this allusion to describe the desperate hope of the Chinese people for peace, in the 1920s. Their hope became a "dream of yellow grain" once more, when Chiang and the warlords fought again.

红旗跃过汀江，直下龙岩上杭。收拾金瓯一片，分田分地真忙。

風雲突變，軍閥重開戰。灑向人間都是怨，一枕黃粱再現。紅旗

Ch'ung   Yang

重阳

Double Yang

Jen   sheng   i,yi   lao   t'ien   nan   lao

人 生 易 老 天 难 老 ，

Man/grow/easy/old/heaven, time/difficulty/old
Man grows old easily but time never

Sui   sui   ch'ung   yang

岁 岁 重 阳 。

Year/year/double/yang
Every year a day of double yang

Chin   yu   ch'ung   yang

今 又 重 阳 ，

Today/again/double/yang
Today is double yang day again

Chan   ti   huang   hua   fen   wai   hsiang

战 地 黄 花 分 外 香 。

War/ground/yellow/flower/share/outside/fragrant
In the battlefield the yellow flowers are exceptionally fragrant

29

I,yi nien i,yi tu ch'iu feng ching

一 年 一 度 秋 风 劲，

One/year/one/time/autumn/wind/strong
Once a year the autumn wind lashes fiercely

Pu szu ch'un kuang

不 似 春 光 。

Not/like/spring/light
It is not like the spring season

Sheng szu ch'un kuang

胜 似 春 光 ，

Better/like/spring/light
It is better than spring

Liao-k'uo chiang t'ien wan li shuang

寥 廓 江 天 万 里 霜 。

Firmament/river/sky/10,000/miles/frost
Clear sky, water, and 10,000 miles of frost

Double Yang

Man ages easily, but time never.
And there is one day of double *yang* every year.
Today that day comes again,
The yellow flower in the battlefield
Is more fragrant than anywhere else.

Once a year autumn winds lash fiercely.
It is not like spring, but
It is better than spring.
Under the clear sky lie
Ten thousand miles of frost and water.

Chinese numbers were conventionally divided into *yin* and *yang* (even and odd). In the old Chinese calendar, the ninth day of the ninth lunar month, a "double nine" day, is the double *yang* day. It is a day of great festivity, celebrated by climbing hills, feasting on persimmons, and showing off chrysanthemums.

Liao-k'uo, in the last line, is a classic compound meaning "vast expanse," "dome of heaven," or "clear expanse of sky."

In classical Chinese, the terms hundred, thousand, or ten thousand are all commonly used to denote large numbers. *Wan* ("ten thousand") *li* could be translated "ten thousand leagues" or "ten thousand miles"—since *li*, like league and mile, in everyday usage is an inexact measurement for a great distance.

风流人物
还看今朝
如此多娇
寒庐
江山
雪。

人生易老天难老，岁岁重阳。今又重阳，战地黄花分外香。一年一度秋

会昌

Hweichang

Tung　fang　yü　hsiao

东 方 欲 晓,

East/direction/about to/dawn
In the east, day begins to dawn

Mo　tao　chün　hsing　tsao

莫 道 君 行 早。

Not/say/you/walk/early
Don't say you travel early

T'a　pien　ch'ing　shan　jen　wei　lao

踏 遍 青 山 人 未 老,

Tramp/all over/green/mountains/man/not/old
Tramp all over green mountains before man is old

Feng-ching　che　pien　tu　hao

风 景 这 边 独 好。

Scenery/this/side/unique/good
The scenery on this side is uniquely beautiful

Hui-ch'ang   ch'eng   wai   kao   feng

会 昌 城 外 高 峰 ，

Hweichang/city/outside/high/peak
The high peak outside the city of Hweichang

Tien   lien   chih-chieh   tung   ming

颠 连 直 接 东 溟 。

Undulate/connect/direct/east/coast
Connects undulatingly all the way to the east coast

Chan-shih   chih   k'an   nan   Yüeh

战 士 指 看 南 粤 ，

Warrior/point/look/south/Yüeh
The warriors aim at south Kwangtung

Keng   chia   yü   yü   ts'ung   ts'ung

更 加 郁 郁 葱 葱 。

Further/more/brilliant/luxuriant green
A brilliantly luxuriant green land

六月天兵征腐恶，万丈长缨要把鲲鹏缚。赣水那边红一角，偏师借重黄公略。

百万工农齐踊跃，席卷江西直捣湘和鄂。国际悲歌歌一曲，狂飙为我从天落。

调寄蝶恋花

一九三○年七月

Hweichang

Day breaks in the east;
Don't say we march too early,
For we'll cover all green hills before we grow old.
The view from here is singularly beautiful.
The crest outside the town of Hweichang
Snakes east to the seaboard.
The warriors aim south toward Kwangtung,
What a luxuriant evergreen land.

1934 on Hweichang Mountain

This poem, like "Chiang Battles in Kwangsi," was written when Chiang Kai-shek was fighting the warlords in Kwangsi and the Red Army was advancing from Kiangsi toward Fukien, a coastal province on the southeastern seaboard. Hweichang is a border town between Kiangsi and Fukien.

Lou   Shan   Kuan

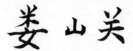

姜 山 关

Loushan Pass

Hsi   feng   lieh

西 风 烈 ，

West/wind/fierce
West wind blows fiercely

Ch'ang-k'ung   yen   chiao   shuang   ch'en   yüeh

长 空 雁 叫 霜 晨 月 。

Long sky, air/geese/call/frost/morning/moonlit
In the sky, geese call in the frosty morning moonlit

Shuang   ch'en   yüeh

霜 晨 月 ，

Frost/morning/moon
Frosty morning moon

Ma   t'i   sheng   sui

马 蹄 声 碎 ，

Horse/hoof/sound/break
The horse's hoofs sound broken

La-pa   sheng   yen

喇 叭 声 咽 。

Bugle/sound/sob
The bugles sound sobbing

Hsiung-kuan   man   tao   chen   ju   t'ieh

雄 关 漫 道 真 如 铁 ，

Strong/pass/don't/say/real/like/iron
Don't complain the fortified pass is hard as iron

Erh-chin   mai   pu   ts'ung   t'ou   yüeh

而 今 迈 步 从 头 越 。

At present/stride/step/from/head/go over
Now stride over it from the first step

Ts'ung   t'ou   yüeh

从 头 越 ，

From/head/go over
From the first step

Ts'ang   shan   ju   hai

苍 山 如 海 ，

Blue/mountain/like/sea
Blue mountains are like sea

Ts'an   yang   ju   hsüeh

残 阳 如 血 。

Decline/sun/like/blood
Dying sun like blood

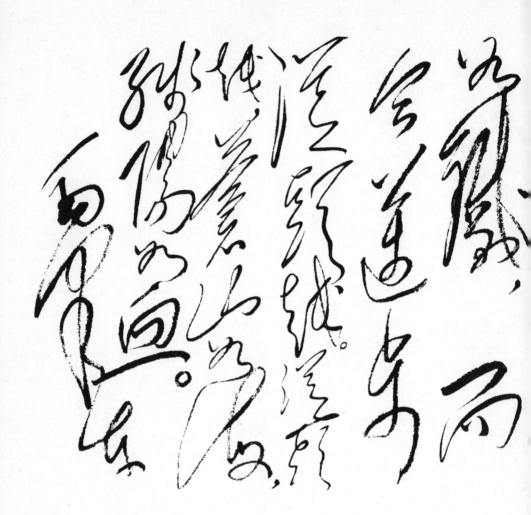

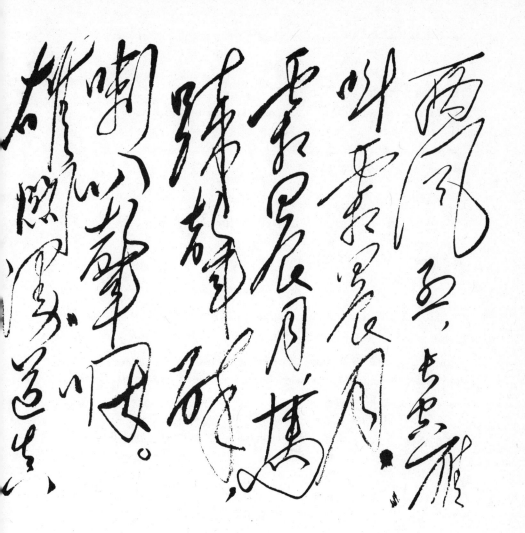

西風烈，長空雁叫霜晨月。霜晨月，馬蹄聲碎，喇叭聲咽。雄關漫道真如鐵，

Loushan Pass

The west wind lashes fiercely.
In the sky the geese honk in the frosty morning moonlit
The frosty morning moonlit
Hoofs clank a broken rhyme,
Bugles wail a mournful tune.

Do not say the defense of the pass is ironclad.
This very day we'll stride over it from the first step.
From the first step,
The blue mountains are like sea,
The dying sun is like blood.

Loushan Pass is north of Tsunyi, in Kweichow Province. In January 1935, the Chinese Communist party held a conference there, and Mao was elected Chairman of the Politburo.

In Chinese, this poem reads as a melodious staccato. The images are in sharp focus. It titillates the Oriental palate for literature which has a slight tinge of sadness.

Chang   Cheng

Long/Expedition

Long March

Hung   chün   pu   p'a   yüan   cheng   nan

红 军 不 怕 远 征 难，

Red/Army/not/afraid/far/expedition/hardship

The Red Army is not afraid of the hardship of long march

Wan   shui   ch'ien   shan   chih   teng   hsien

万 水 千 山 只 等 闲 。

Ten thousand/water/thousand/mountain/only/wait/leisure

Ten thousand rivers and a thousand mountains are waiting for our leisure

Wu-ling   wei   i, yi   t'eng   hsi   lang

五 岭 逶 迤 腾 细 浪，

Wuling/winding/extending/fly/fine/wave

Wuling ranges are winding and extending like fine flying ripples

Wu-meng   pang-po   tsou   ni   wan

乌 蒙 磅 礴 走 泥 丸 。

Wumeng/vast/walk/clay/bead

Vast Wumeng is like a rolling bead of clay

45

Chin sha shui p'ai yün yai nuan

金沙水拍云崖暖，

Gold/sand/water/pat/cloud/cliff/warm
Gold Sand water pats the warm cliff rising high into the cloud

Ta-tu ch'iao heng t'ieh so han

大渡桥横铁索寒。

Tatu/Bridge/cross/iron/chain/cold
The iron chain cross over Tatu Bridge is cold

Keng hsi min shan ch'ien li hsüeh

更喜岷山千里雪，

More/happy/Min/Mountain/thousand/miles/snow
A thousand miles of snow on the Min Mountain is a happy sight

San chün kuo hou chin k'ai yen

三军过后尽开颜。

Three/army/cross/after/all/open/face
Soldiers, after crossing, all open faces

The Long March

The Red Army is fearless of the hardship of the Long March.
Myriad rivers and mountains are only there for us to conquer.
The Wuling ranges ripple like a fine spray,
Majestic Wumeng rolls only a bead of clay.
Gold Sand River laps the warm cliffs wrapped in the clouds,
The chain of iron across the Tatu River locks up the bitter cold.
We are happy amid the endless snow on the Min Mountain, but
Happier are the smiling faces of soldiers after crossing over it.

April 20, 1962

This poem was written in October 1935, when the Long March crossed over the Gold Sand River in Szechwan on the way to Kansu, but the inscription in calligraphy is dated April 20, 1962.

Wuling ("five ranges"): there are five famous mountain ranges in China, the Tayu, Tupang, Mengchu, Chitien, and Chengyueh Ling. They span five provinces, Kiangsi, Hunan, Fukien, Kwangtung, and Kwangsi.

The Tatu River is a tributary of the Yangtze, on the border of Szechwan and Sikang. The bridge mentioned in the poem is at Luting.

In the last line, the army, literally translated, is three (*san chün*): the First, Second, and Fourth Front armies. In the Chou dynasty (1125-1255 B.C.), a large state possessed three armies of 37,500 men, but in contemporary usage *san chün* refers to army in general.

In the sixth line, *han* means "cold" or "poor," but "bitter" is added here for parallel construction and contrast with "warm cliffs" in the fifth line. This poem is written in the Lü Shih (regulated) style with seven characters per line, whose restrictive form requires parallelism and contrast.

……拍云崖暖，大渡桥横铁索寒。更喜岷山千里雪，三军过后尽开颜。

毛泽东

一九六三年十二月

长征诗一首

红军不怕远征难,万水千山只等闲。五岭逶迤腾细浪,乌蒙磅礴走泥丸。金沙水

Luting Bridge over the Tatu River.
The Red Army captured it during the Long March.

Liu P'an Shan

六 盘 山

Six-Spiral/Mountain
Liu P'an Mountain

T'ien kao yün tan

天 高 云 淡，

Sky/high/cloud/light
Sky high cloud light

Wang tuan nan fei yen

望 断 南 飞 雁 。

Look/break/south/fly/geese
Geese fly south, disappear from sight

Pu tao ch'ang ch'eng fei hao han

不 到 长 城 非 好 汉，

Not/reach/long/wall/not/good/fellow
Don't reach the Great Wall, won't be a good man

Ch'ü chih hsing ch'eng erh wan

屈 指 行 程 二 万 。

Bend/finger/travel/distance/two/ten thousand
Counting on fingers, traveled twenty thousand miles

Liu p'an shan shang kao feng

六盘山上高峰，

Six/spiral/mountain/up, top/high/peak
On top of the high peak of Six-Spiral Mountain

Hung ch'i man chüan hsi feng

红旗漫卷西风。

Red/banner/overflow/roll/west/wind
The red banner billows in the west wind

Chin-jih ch'ang ying tsai shou

今日长缨在手，

Today/long/cord/at/hand
Today hold the long cord in hand

Ho shih fu-chu ts'ang lung

何时缚住苍龙？

What/time/bind (bound)/green/dragon
When capture the green dragon

Liupan Mountain

High in the light cloud sky
The geese fly south out of sight.
He who fails to reach the Great Wall will not be a hero.
Counting on fingers, we have marched twenty thousand miles.

On the high peaks of Liupan Mountain
Red banners billow in the west wind.
Today we are holding the long cord in hand.
When shall we capture the green dragon?

Liupan Shan, or Six-Spiral Mountain, is in Kansu. It is so high and steep that the road to the summit spirals six times around it. Toward the end of the Long March, on October 7, 1935, the First Front Army, under the leadership of Mao, captured Liupan and advanced into Shensi, where Yenan is situated.

The long cord: during the Han dynasty (A.D. 206—20), Chung Chun asked Wu Ti, the emperor, for a long cord with which he pledged to capture the king of South Yüeh, who was leading the barbarians in an invasion of the country. The king of South Yüeh was symbolized by the green dragon; Mao may be alluding here to the invading Japanese, or to other evils in China.

天高雲淡，
望斷南飛雁。
不到長城非好漢，
屈指行程二
萬。

六盤
山上高峰，
紅旗漫卷

Yu Yung

游泳

Swimming

Ts'ai   yin   ch'ang-sha   shui

才饮长沙水，

Just/drink/Ch'angsha/water
Just drank Changsha water

Yu   shih   wu-ch'ang   yü

又食武昌鱼。

Again/eat/Wuchang/fish
Again eat Wuchang fish

Wan   li   ch'ang   chiang   heng   tu

万里长江横渡，

Ten thousand/mile/long/river/crosswise/ferry
Ferry across ten thousand mile long river

Chi   mu   ch'u   t'ien   shu

极目楚天舒。

To reach end of/eye/Hunan/sky/stretch out
The southern sky stretches out as far as eyes can see

Pu   kuan   feng   ch'ui   lang   ta

不 管 风 吹 浪 打，

Don't/care/wind/blow/wave/strike
Don't care the wind blows and waves strike

Sheng   szu   hsien   t'ing   hsin   pu

胜 似 闲 庭 信 步，

Better/like/leisure/courtyard/easy of mind/step
Better than a stroll in a courtyard

Chin-jih   te   k'uan   yü

今 日 得 宽 馀。

Today/gain/wide/surplus
Today gain wide space

Tzu   tsai   ch'uan   shang   yüeh

子 在 川 上 曰：

Master/at/river/upon/said
The Master said by a riverbank

Shih-che   ju   szu   fu

逝 者 如 斯 夫！

That which passed away/as/this (a final particle)
That which passed away is like this (what is flowing on)

Feng   ch'iang   tung

风 樯 动,

Wind/mast/move
The wind moves the sail

Kuei   she   ching

龟 蛇 静,

Turtle/Snake/still
The Turtle and the Snake (hills) still

Ch'i   hung   t'u

起 宏 图。

Arise/grand/plan
Great plans come up

Yi   ch'iao   fei   chia   nan   pei

一 桥 飞 架 南 北,

One/bridge/fly/support/south/north
A bridge flies across the south and the north

T'ien   ch'ien   pien   t'ung   t'u

天 堑 变 通 途。

Sky, nature/barrier/change/through/road
Nature's barrier changes into a thoroughfare

61

Keng li hsi chiang shih pi

更立西江石壁，

Again/stand/west/river/rock/cliff, wall
Build a dam to the west of the river

Chieh tuan wu shan yün yü

截断巫山云雨，

Obstruct/break/Wu/mountain/cloud/rain
Block the rainfall from the Wu Mountain

Kao hsia ch'u p'ing hu

高峡出平湖。

High/gorge/come out/smooth/lake
High gorge comes into calm lake

Shen-nü ying wu yang

神女应无恙，

Goddess/should/no/harm
No harm done to goddess

Tang ching shih-chieh shu

当惊世界殊。

Ought to/surprise/world/different
Ought to be surprised by the changing world

Swimming

Having just swallowed Changsha water,
I am now tasting Wuchang fish.
While I am swimming across the ten-thousand-mile long Yangtze River,
The southern sky stretches out as far as my eyes can see.
I don't care how the winds blow and waves strike.
This is better than strolling in a courtyard.
Today I feel free in this wide space.
Standing by the river, the Master said,
"What has passed by was like this."

The wind moves the sail.
Tortoise Mountain and Snake Hill stand still.
Great projects are planned for here.
A bridge flies across the river from north to south,
Nature's barrier becomes a throughway.
Build a dam upstream in the west,
It will hold the rainfall from the mountain region of Wu,
Torrents from high gorges will empty into calm lakes.
These projects should not harm the goddess, but
She will certainly be surprised by the changing world.

December 5, 1956

The second line of the poem refers to Mao's famous swim across the Yangtze River in May 1956, when he was sixty-two years old. The calligraphic version is dated December 5, 1956.

Ch'u sky: during the period of the Three Warring States (474-221 B.C.), the kingdom of Ch'u was in what is now Hunan Province, To swim across the Yangtze River from Hankow to Wuchang, as Mao did, one has to face south toward Ch'u. Ch'u sky is therefore freely translated as "southern sky."

The Master referred to at the end of the first stanza is Confucius (551-479 B.C.), and the quotation is from the Analects. An interpretation of the line would be, "Life flows into the past like the river."

南北天堑变通途。

立西江石壁，截断巫山

云雨，高峡出平湖。神女

应无恙，当惊世界

殊。

水调歌头
游泳

才饮长沙水，又食武昌鱼。万里长江横渡，极目楚天舒。不管风吹浪打，胜似闲庭信步，今日得宽馀。子在川上曰：逝者如斯夫！

风樯动，龟蛇静，起宏图。一桥飞架

Wu Mountain is on the border of Szechwan and Hupeh, where three famous gorges narrow down the upper Yangtze River into an almost impassable waterway. From this point on, boats have to be towed by manpower. Po Chü-I, in his poem, "Alarm at First Entering the Yangtze Gorge," wrote, "Above, mountains ten thousand feet high, below, a river ten thousand feet deep" (A.D. 818). Li Po, in his poem, "Pathway to Shu" (Szechwan), wrote, "The waterway to Shu is difficult, more difficult than climbing the blue heaven."

The goddess of Wu referred to in the last lines appears in a story narrated in the preface to the "Kaotang Fu," a poem by Sung Yü. On a visit to Kaotang, King Hsiang of Ch'u (294-264 B.C.) napped in the afternoon and dreamed that he had sexual intercourse with a beautiful woman. When she left him, she said that she lived on the *yang* (south) side of Wu Mountain and her duty was to see to it that there were clouds in the morning and rain in the evening. She was said to be the goddess of Wu. Thus, in classic Chinese literature, Wu Shan connotes a place of rendezous for lovers and cloud-rain alludes to sexual love. In fact, the Wu Shan region is a fertile farming area, rich in rainfall.

Wei Li Chin T'ung Chih

为 李 进 同 志

For/Li/Chin/Comrade

T'i So She Lu-shan

题 所 摄 庐 山

inscript/by/photograph/Lushan

Hsien-jen Tung Chao

仙 人 洞 照

immortal/cave/photography

Mu se ts'ang-mang k'an ching sung

暮 色 苍 茫 看 劲 松 ，

Evening/color/vast dark blue/see/strong/pine tree
Seen in the dark blue evening light are these stately pine trees

Luan yün fei tu jeng ts'ung-jung

乱 云 飞 渡 仍 从 容 。

Disorder/cloud/fly/ferry/still/ with/easy
Scattered clouds flow among these trees with ease

T'ien sheng yi-ko hsien-jen tung

天 生 一 个 仙 人 洞 ，

Nature/birth/one/immortal/cave
Nature produces a cave of immortals

Wu-hsien feng kuang tsai hsien feng

无 限 风 光 在 险 峰 。

Limitless/wind/light/at/danger/peak
Matchless scenery at a dangerous crag

Inscription on a Photograph of the Cave of the Immortals, Lushan, Taken by Comrade Li Chin

Wrapped in the dark blue evening light, these stately pine trees.
Scattered clouds flow among them with ease.
Nature chisels a cave for the immortals
In this matchless beauty of perilous crag.

Lushan is a summer resort at Kiukiang, Kiangsi. One of its famous sites is the Cave of the Immortals, a Taoist shrine.

无限风光在险峰。

一九六一年九月

暮色苍茫看劲松，乱云飞渡仍从容。天生一个仙人洞，无限风光在险峰。